TOKYO TRAVEL

GUIDE FOR KIDS

Everything You Need To Know About Tokyo
Before Travelling With Your Children

Sarah Wiseman

TABLE OF CONTENT

INTRODUCTION

In a bustling household with four excited kids, the idea of a family trip to Tokyo took shape. The kids' eyes sparkled with anticipation as we discussed the possibilities of exploring the vibrant city together. Little did I know that this adventure would not only become one of the most cherished memories of our lives but also inspire me to create a Tokyo Travel Guide for Kids.

With passports in hand and hearts filled with excitement, we boarded the plane bound for Tokyo. As the plane touched down at Haneda Airport, the kids were wide-eyed, taking in the sights and sounds of this bustling metropolis.

Our first stop was the iconic Tokyo Tower, standing tall against the skyline. The kids were amazed by the panoramic views from the observation deck, and we even spotted some famous landmarks like the Tokyo Skytree in the distance. The tower's bright orange color left an impression that would stay with us throughout the trip.

Next on our list was a visit to the magical world of Tokyo Disneyland. The kids couldn't contain their joy as they met beloved Disney characters and enjoyed thrilling rides. The enchanting parades and dazzling fireworks lit up their faces with pure delight. Watching the kids immersed in their favorite fairytales was a heartwarming sight.

Our journey through Tokyo's neighborhoods was a delight in itself. Asakusa with its traditional charm, Shinjuku's vibrant lights, and Harajuku's quirky fashion scene all left an impression on the kids. The bustling streets, colorful shops, and friendly locals made them feel right at home in this diverse city.

Of course, we couldn't miss out on the unique Japanese cuisine. The kids tried sushi for the first time at a conveyor belt sushi restaurant, and their faces lit up with surprise and joy as they experienced this delicious novelty. We also indulged in delightful street food like takoyaki and taiyaki, which the kids couldn't get enough of.

One of the highlights of our trip was visiting the Ghibli Museum. The kids were entranced by the world of Studio Ghibli, and they explored the enchanting exhibits with wonder in their eyes. From the Catbus to the life-sized Totoro, it was like stepping into their favorite animated films.

As the days passed, our adventures continued with visits to Ueno Park, where we picnicked under the cherry blossoms, and the interactive exhibits at the National Museum of Nature and Science, which sparked the kids' curiosity about the world around them.

At the end of our trip, with memories to last a lifetime, we returned home with hearts full of joy and a deep love for Tokyo. It was during our journey that I realized the immense potential of Tokyo as a family-friendly destination. Inspired by the smiles and laughter of my kids, I decided to create a Tokyo Travel Guide for Kids to help other families embark on their own unforgettable adventures.

Putting pen to paper, I poured my heart into crafting a comprehensive guide that would be a valuable resource for parents and a delightful companion for young travelers. I included details on the best family-friendly attractions, tips for navigating the city with kids, and insights into the rich cultural experiences Tokyo has to offer.

As I wrote, the memories of our Tokyo trip flooded back, and I wanted every family to experience the magic we had felt. The guide became a labor of love, a testament to the joy and wonder that Tokyo brought to our lives.

Today, as I reflect on that incredible journey, I am filled with gratitude for the unforgettable experiences we shared as a family. Tokyo ignited a sense of adventure in my kids' hearts, and through the Tokyo Travel Guide for Kids, I hope to inspire many more families to embark on their own extraordinary journeys to this magical city. Tokyo will forever hold a special place in our hearts, and the guide is my way of sharing that love with the world, one family at a time.

Welcome to Tokyo!

Tokyo, the bustling capital of Japan, is a fascinating city filled with a perfect blend of ancient traditions and modern marvels. It's a fantastic destination for families with kids, offering an array of attractions and activities that cater specifically to young travelers. As you embark on your Tokyo adventure, here's what you need to know:

1. Vibrant Culture and Traditions: Tokyo is steeped in rich cultural heritage, and exploring its customs can be an enriching experience for kids. From the elaborate art of origami to the graceful tea ceremonies, Tokyo's traditional practices provide an insight into Japan's fascinating past.

2. Kid-Friendly Atmosphere: Tokyo is a remarkably safe and family-friendly city. The locals are warm, courteous, and often delighted to interact with children, making it a comfortable environment for families to explore.

3. Transportation Convenience: Tokyo boasts an efficient and extensive public transportation system, including subways and trains. Although it might seem daunting initially, it's surprisingly easy to navigate with kids. You can purchase IC cards like Suica or Pasmo, which allow hassle-free entry on trains and buses.

4. Language Considerations: While many people in Tokyo can understand basic English, it's useful to learn a few essential Japanese phrases. Locals appreciate the effort and will gladly help you if needed.

5. Weather and Seasonal Considerations: Tokyo experiences distinct seasons, each with its charm. Spring brings cherry blossoms, while summers can be warm and humid. Fall is marked by colorful foliage, and winters can be chilly.Prior to your journey, make sure you pack appropriately and check the weather prediction.

6. Must-Visit Attractions: Tokyo offers a wide range of attractions that captivate kids' imaginations. Some iconic places to include on your itinerary are Tokyo Disneyland, where beloved Disney characters come to life, and the Tokyo Skytree, a towering observation deck providing stunning city views.

7. Parks and Playgrounds: Tokyo is home to several beautiful parks and playgrounds that offer ample space for kids to run, play, and picnic. Popular choices include Ueno Park, Yoyogi Park, and Shinjuku Gyoen National Garden.

8. Unique Experiences: Don't miss the chance to visit the Ghibli Museum, dedicated to the legendary Studio Ghibli's animated

films, or the Tokyo Toy Museum, showcasing a vast collection of toys from around the world.

9. Food Adventures: Japanese cuisine is a treat for the taste buds, and Tokyo boasts a plethora of kid-friendly dining options. Try conveyor belt sushi (kaiten-zushi) restaurants, themed cafes with adorable character dishes, and delightful street food.

10. Safety and Security: Tokyo is known for its low crime rate and safety. However, it's essential to keep a close eye on your children, especially in crowded areas, and teach them about safety measures like crossing roads and using public transport.

About This Guide

This comprehensive Tokyo Travel Guide for Kids aims to provide families with valuable information to plan an unforgettable trip. With detailed insights into the city's attractions, activities, dining, and more, this guide seeks to ensure that your Tokyo experience is enjoyable, memorable, and stress-free.

1. Purpose and Scope: The primary purpose of this guide is to cater specifically to families traveling to Tokyo with kids. It covers a wide range of topics, including kid-friendly attractions, safety considerations, cultural experiences, dining options, and practical tips to make the most of your journey.

2. Personalized Recommendations: Recognizing that each family is unique, this guide offers personalized recommendations based on various interests and age groups. Whether you have curious preschoolers or adventurous teenagers, you'll find tailored suggestions to suit every child's preferences.

3. Cultural Awareness: Understanding the local culture is crucial for any travel experience. This guide includes cultural insights to help parents and kids navigate Tokyo's customs, etiquettes, and traditions with respect and appreciation.

4. Travel Logistics: Planning a family trip can be challenging, especially when children are involved. This guide provides essential information on transportation, accommodation options, and language considerations to ensure a smooth journey.

5. Practical Tips: Traveling with kids requires careful preparation, and this guide offers a range of practical tips and advice to enhance your experience. From packing essentials to dealing with jet lag, every aspect of your trip is considered.

Tips for a Fun and Safe Trip

A memorable and enjoyable trip to Tokyo with kids is achievable with proper preparation and a focus on safety. Here are some valuable tips to ensure your adventure is fun-filled and stress-free:

1. Pre-Trip Planning:

Involve your kids in the planning process. Let them research attractions and activities to build excitement.

Create an itinerary that balances child-friendly attractions, parks, and cultural experiences.

Check the weather forecast and pack appropriate clothing for your visit.

2. Safety First:

Discuss safety rules with your kids and set clear boundaries for exploring the city.

Use child safety harnesses or wristbands in crowded areas to keep young children close.

Carry identification for your children, including emergency contact information.

3. Public Transportation:

Familiarize yourself with Tokyo's public transportation system before your trip.

Opt for child-friendly seating areas on trains, which often have designated spaces for families.

Have a map and route plan readily available for easy navigation.

4. Hydration and Snacks:

Keep your kids hydrated, especially during the hot and humid summer months.

Carry snacks and small treats to keep their energy levels up during sightseeing.

5. Cultural Experiences:

Introduce your kids to Japanese customs and traditions before arriving in Tokyo.

Encourage them to try local foods and participate in interactive workshops.

6. Language Considerations:

Teach your kids basic Japanese phrases for greetings and expressions of gratitude.

Use translation apps or phrasebooks to facilitate communication.

7. Photographic Memories:

Document your journey with photographs to create lasting memories for your kids.

Let your children take pictures too, capturing moments from their perspective.

8. Be Flexible:

Understand that traveling with kids can be unpredictable, and flexibility is key.

Be prepared to adapt your plans if needed and prioritize the enjoyment of your family.

9. Rest and Relaxation:

Pace your itinerary to include breaks for rest and relaxation, especially for young children.

Utilize green spaces and parks for leisurely breaks.

10. Embrace the Joy of Discovery:

Encourage curiosity and exploration in your kids as they encounter new sights and experiences.

Emphasize the joy of discovery rather than rushing through attractions. By following these tips, you can create an unforgettable Tokyo travel experience for your kids, fostering a love for exploration, culture, and adventure that will last a lifetime. Remember to prioritize their safety, engage them in the journey, and have fun discovering the wonders of Tokyo together!

CHAPTER 1

Getting Ready for Tokyo

Preparing for the Trip

Preparing for a family trip to Tokyo requires careful planning and organization. By taking the time to consider essential aspects of your journey, you can ensure a smooth and enjoyable travel experience for everyone involved. Here are some crucial steps to take when preparing for your Tokyo adventure with kids:

1. Setting the Travel Dates:

Choose travel dates that align with school holidays or a time convenient for your family's schedule.

Consider seasonal factors, such as weather and popular events, to enhance your experience.

2. Researching Tokyo:

Familiarize yourself with Tokyo's top attractions and family-friendly activities.

Research the cultural aspects of the city to ensure you have an understanding of its customs.

3. Budgeting and Financial Planning:

Create a travel budget that includes expenses for transportation, accommodation, food, attractions, and souvenirs.

Consider additional costs for unexpected expenses and emergencies.

4. Booking Accommodation:

Choose family-friendly accommodation that offers amenities catering to children, such as play areas or swimming pools.

Book your accommodation well in advance to secure the best rates and availability.

5. Organizing Travel Documents:

Ensure all family members have valid passports with at least six months of validity beyond the travel dates.

Check visa requirements for Japan based on your nationality and apply for visas, if necessary.

6. Vaccinations and Health Considerations:

Consult your healthcare provider or a travel clinic for recommended vaccinations before traveling to Japan.

Carry necessary medications and a first aid kit for any potential health issues.

7. Travel Insurance:

Invest in comprehensive travel insurance that includes coverage for unexpected circumstances like medical crises and trip cancellations.

8. Packing for the Trip:

Create a packing list for each family member, including clothing, toiletries, and other essentials.

Pack light, but ensure you have enough clothing for different weather conditions.

9. Entertainment for Kids:

Bring along entertainment options for kids during travel, such as coloring books, puzzles, and electronic devices with headphones.

10. Language Considerations:

Familiarize yourself and your kids with basic Japanese phrases for communication.

Carry a pocket-sized phrasebook or use translation apps for easy interactions.

11. Planning Itinerary:

Create a flexible and well-balanced itinerary that includes a mix of kid-friendly attractions, cultural experiences, and free time for relaxation.

Consider the energy levels and interests of your children when planning daily activities.

12. Safety Precautions:

Teach your kids about safety rules, especially in crowded areas and when using public transportation.

Establish a meeting point in case anyone gets separated during outings.

13. Sharing Responsibilities:

Involve your children in age-appropriate trip preparations to make them feel included and responsible.

14. Informing Schools and Others:

If your kids will be missing school, inform the school authorities in advance and arrange for any necessary assignments or homework.

15. Double-Checking Details:

Double-check all travel reservations, documents, and important information before departure.

Travel Documents and Visa Requirements

Before traveling to Tokyo, it's crucial to ensure that all required travel documents are in order. Here's what you need to know about travel documents and visa requirements for your trip:

1. Passport:

A valid passport is a must for all travelers to Tokyo, including children and infants.

Check the passport's expiration date and ensure it remains valid for at least six months beyond your intended departure date.

2. Visa Requirements:

Japan has visa exemption agreements with many countries. However, some nationalities may require a visa to enter Japan.

Check the official website of the Japanese embassy or consulate in your country to determine the visa requirements for your nationality.

3. Tourist Visa:

If a visa is required, apply for a tourist visa well in advance of your travel dates.

Tourist visas typically allow a stay of up to 90 days for leisure purposes.

4. Visa Application Process:

Gather all required documents for the visa application, which may include passport-sized photos, a completed application form, travel itinerary, and proof of accommodation.

Submit the visa application to the nearest Japanese embassy or consulate and pay any applicable fees.

5. Visa Processing Time:

Visa processing times may vary depending on the embassy or consulate and the time of year. It's advisable to apply for the visa well ahead of your intended travel date.

6. Multiple-Entry Visas:

Some travelers may require a multiple-entry visa if they plan to leave and re-enter Japan during their trip. Check visa requirements for specific details.

7. Visas for Non-Resident Family Members:

If you are traveling with family members who are not residents of the same country as you, they may have different visa requirements. Ensure they obtain the necessary visas for Japan.

8. Visa Extensions:

Tourist visas are typically non-extendable. If you plan to stay in Japan for an extended period, consider other visa options or exit and re-enter the country.

9. Electronic Travel Authorization (ETA):

Some countries may offer Electronic Travel Authorizations (ETAs) or visa waivers for short-term visits to Japan. Check if this option applies to your nationality.

10. Emergency Travel Documents:

If your passport is lost or stolen while in Tokyo, contact your country's embassy or consulate for assistance in obtaining an emergency travel document.

Packing Essentials for Kids

Packing for a trip to Tokyo with kids requires thoughtful consideration of their specific needs and preferences. Here's a comprehensive list of essential items to ensure a comfortable and enjoyable journey:

1. Travel Documents:

Passports for all family members, including children.

Airline tickets or e-tickets.

Printed copies of hotel reservations and travel itineraries.

Any required visas or travel authorization documents.

2. Clothing:

Comfortable and weather-appropriate clothing for each family member.

Lightweight and breathable clothes for the summer months, and warm layers for cooler seasons.

Rain jackets or umbrellas for rainy days.

Swimsuits if your accommodation has a pool or if you plan to visit water parks.

3. Footwear:

Comfortable walking shoes for sightseeing and exploring.

Sandals or flip-flops for warm weather.

Closed-toe shoes suitable for hiking or more adventurous activities.

4. Toiletries and Personal Care:

Travel-sized toiletries, including shampoo, conditioner, soap, and toothpaste.

Sunscreen with a high SPF suitable for kids.

Insect repellent to protect against mosquitoes, especially during summer.

5. Medications and First Aid:

Any necessary prescription medications for each family member.

A basic first aid kit containing band-aids, antiseptic cream, pain relievers, and medications for common ailments like colds and allergies.

6. Travel Gear for Kids:

Lightweight strollers or baby carriers for young children.

Portable high chair or booster seat for dining at restaurants.

Diapers, wipes, and baby essentials for infants and toddlers.

7. Entertainment and Snacks:

Books, coloring books, and activity pads to keep kids entertained during travel.

Electronic devices with headphones for movies, games, or educational apps.

Snacks and drinks to keep kids energized during long journeys.

8. Travel Adapters and Chargers:

Universal travel adapters to charge electronic devices.

Portable chargers to keep devices powered on the go.

9. Reusable Water Bottles:

Stay hydrated during sightseeing by carrying reusable water bottles for the whole family.

10. Backpacks or Day Bags:

Comfortable and spacious backpacks or day bags to carry essentials during outings.

11. Safety Items:

Child safety harnesses or wristbands for crowded areas.

Identification cards with emergency contact information for children.

12. Weather-Specific Gear:

Winter clothing, including warm jackets, gloves, and hats, for visits during the colder months.

Summer essentials, such as hats and sunglasses, to protect against the sun.

13. Laundry Supplies:

Laundry detergent or travel-sized laundry sheets to wash clothes during your trip.

14. Translation Tools:

Pocket-sized language translation books or translation apps to help with communication.

15. Snacks and Special Foods:

Pack familiar snacks and any special foods your kids may prefer, especially for picky eaters.

Understanding Japanese Culture and Customs

Understanding Japanese culture and customs is essential to ensure a respectful and enjoyable trip to Tokyo. By embracing the local traditions and etiquette, you can make the most of your experience and foster positive interactions with the Japanese people. Here are some key aspects of Japanese culture and customs to keep in mind:

1. Bowing:

Bowing is a common greeting in Japan, and it is essential to show respect when meeting someone for the first time or in a formal setting.

Teach your kids the appropriate way to bow as a gesture of politeness.

2. Greetings:

Japanese people often use specific greetings depending on the time of day. During the day, "Konnichiwa" is used to say "hello," while "Konbanwa," which means "good evening," is used at night.

3. Removing Shoes Indoors:

In Japanese homes, certain accommodations, and many traditional places like temples, it is customary to remove shoes before entering.

Be prepared to remove your shoes and follow the host's lead when visiting someone's home or specific establishments.

4. Gift Giving:

Gift-giving is an important part of Japanese culture. If invited to someone's home, bringing a small gift or souvenir from your home country is a thoughtful gesture.

Avoid giving gifts in sets of four, as the number four is associated with bad luck in Japan.

5. Public Behavior:

Japanese society places a strong emphasis on maintaining harmony and respect for others in public spaces.

Encourage your children to maintain quiet and orderly behavior when visiting public places like museums, parks, and temples.

6. Use of Chopsticks:

If you dine at restaurants serving Japanese cuisine, your kids may encounter chopsticks.

Familiarize them with basic chopstick etiquette, such as not sticking chopsticks upright in rice (as it resembles a funeral ritual) and not passing food directly from one pair of chopsticks to another.

7. Politeness and Respect:

Japanese culture values politeness and respect in interactions with others.

Teach your kids to say "Arigatou" (thank you) and "Sumimasen" (excuse me) to express gratitude and apologize when appropriate.

8. Quiet Spaces:

Many places in Japan, such as temples and shrines, are considered sacred spaces where silence and contemplation are expected.

Encourage your kids to respect these quiet spaces and avoid running or making loud noises.

9. Bathing Culture:

Japanese culture places significant importance on bathing for relaxation and cleanliness.

If you stay in a traditional ryokan with communal baths, teach your kids about onsen etiquette and bathing procedures.

10. Tipping:

Unlike in some Western countries, tipping is not customary in Japan and may even be considered rude.

You can show appreciation for excellent service with a smile and a "thank you."

11. Taking Photos:

While it's acceptable to take photos in public places, always ask for permission before photographing individuals, especially in private settings.

Be mindful of photography rules in museums and other attractions.

12. Queuing and Waiting in Line:

Japanese people value orderly queuing and waiting in line.

Teach your kids to wait patiently and not push or cut in line at attractions, shops, or public transport.

13. Eating Etiquette:

Encourage your kids to try local Japanese dishes, and teach them basic table manners, such as not talking with a full mouth and saying "Itadakimasu" before starting a meal.

14. Use of Public Transportation:

Trains and buses in Japan are generally quiet, and phone calls are discouraged.

Remind your kids to use headphones when listening to music or watching videos in public places.

15. Understanding "Wa" (Harmony):

"Wa" is a fundamental concept in Japanese culture, emphasizing harmony and a sense of balance.

Encourage your kids to respect the environment, follow rules, and act with consideration for others to promote "wa" during their visit.

By incorporating an understanding of Japanese culture and customs into your trip, you and your kids can embrace the unique traditions of Tokyo, fostering positive interactions with locals and leaving a lasting impression of respect and appreciation for the country's culture.

CHAPTER 2

Where to Stay

Family-Friendly Accommodation Options

Choosing the right accommodation is crucial for a successful and enjoyable family trip to Tokyo. Luckily, the city offers a wide range of family-friendly accommodation options that cater specifically to the needs of young travelers. Here's a detailed overview of the different types of family-friendly accommodation you can consider:

1. Hotels:

Tokyo boasts numerous hotels that are well-suited for families. Many hotels offer family rooms or interconnected rooms, providing enough space for everyone.

Look for hotels with facilities catering to kids, such as playrooms, children's pools, or even on-site childcare services.

Some hotels also provide amenities like baby cots, high chairs, and strollers upon request.

2. Serviced Apartments:

Serviced apartments are an excellent choice for families who prefer the comfort of a home away from home.

These apartments typically come with fully equipped kitchens, separate living areas, and multiple bedrooms, providing ample space for families to relax and unwind.

3. Family-Focused Resorts:

Tokyo is home to a few family-focused resorts that provide all-inclusive packages and a variety of family-friendly activities.

These resorts often have dedicated kids' clubs, water parks, and entertainment options to keep children engaged and entertained.

4. Capsule Hotels with Family Floors:

Some capsule hotels in Tokyo have introduced family floors, where parents and kids can stay together in larger capsules.

These family floors usually offer shared facilities like family bathrooms and common areas.

5. Guesthouses and Hostels:

Family-friendly guesthouses and hostels are a budget-friendly option for families traveling to Tokyo.

Look for private rooms or family dormitories with bunk beds to accommodate the entire family.

6. Theme Hotels:

Tokyo is known for its unique and themed hotels that appeal to kids' imaginations.

Consider staying at a hotel with themes like anime, characters, or popular children's shows for a memorable experience.

7. Onsen Hotels with Family Baths:

For families interested in experiencing traditional Japanese hot springs (onsen), some onsen hotels offer family baths that can be reserved for private use.

This allows families to enjoy the onsen experience together while maintaining privacy.

8. Airbnb and Vacation Rentals:

Many families opt for Airbnb or vacation rentals to have a homely and personalized experience.

These accommodations often come with fully equipped kitchens, allowing families to prepare their meals.

9. Location Considerations:

Choose accommodations located near family-friendly attractions, parks, and public transportation for convenient access to the city's highlights.

Consider the distance to nearby supermarkets or convenience stores for stocking up on snacks and essentials.

10. Safety and Security:

Prioritize accommodations with adequate safety measures, such as childproofing options, secure locks, and 24-hour security.

Check reviews and ratings to ensure that previous guests have had positive experiences, especially when traveling with kids.

Hotels with Kid-Friendly Amenities

Hotels with kid-friendly amenities are designed to provide an enjoyable and comfortable stay for families visiting Tokyo. These amenities cater specifically to children's needs, ensuring that young travelers have a delightful experience throughout their stay. Here are some of the common kid-friendly amenities offered by hotels in Tokyo:

1. Spacious Family Rooms:

Many hotels offer spacious family rooms with multiple beds or interconnected rooms, allowing families to stay together in comfort.

Look for rooms that have enough space for kids to move around freely and play.

2. Children's Playrooms and Activity Areas:

Kid-friendly hotels often have dedicated playrooms or activity areas where children can engage in games, toys, and creative play.

These spaces are supervised and designed to keep kids entertained while parents relax nearby.

3. Kids' Pools and Water Play Areas:

Some hotels feature kids' pools or water play areas with shallow sections and water features suitable for younger children.

Water play areas are perfect for kids to splash and have fun under adult supervision.

4. On-Site Childcare Services:

Luxury hotels may offer on-site childcare services or babysitting options, allowing parents to enjoy some alone time or have a romantic dinner.

5. Kids' Menus in Restaurants:

Family-friendly hotels typically offer kids' menus in their restaurants, providing a selection of child-appropriate dishes and portion sizes.

6. Baby and Toddler Amenities:

Some hotels provide baby cots, high chairs, and strollers upon request, minimizing the need to bring bulky baby equipment.

7. Kids' Clubs and Activities:

Many family-friendly resorts and larger hotels have kids' clubs that organize age-appropriate activities and games for children.

Kids' clubs offer a chance for children to make friends and participate in supervised fun while parents enjoy other aspects of the hotel.

8. In-Room Entertainment:

Hotels often provide in-room entertainment options for kids, such as children's TV channels, DVD players, or video game consoles.

9. Kid-Friendly Concierge Services:

Some hotels have concierge services that can assist with family-friendly recommendations, such as nearby playgrounds, kid-friendly restaurants, or family attractions.

10. Welcome Gifts for Kids:

Some hotels offer welcome gifts or amenities for children upon arrival, making them feel special and excited about their stay.

Traditional Ryokans for an Authentic Experience

For families seeking an authentic cultural experience, staying in a traditional ryokan can be a unique and enriching option. Ryokans are traditional Japanese inns that offer a glimpse into Japan's rich heritage and customs. Here's what you need to know about ryokans and how they cater to families:

1. Japanese Tatami Rooms:

Ryokans feature Japanese-style tatami rooms, where guests sleep on futons laid out on traditional straw mats.

Families can experience sleeping arrangements similar to how Japanese families have done for generations.

2. Onsen (Hot Springs) Baths:

Many ryokans have onsen baths, which are natural hot springs renowned for their therapeutic properties.

Families can soak together in communal or private onsen baths, providing a relaxing experience.

3. Kaiseki Meals:

Ryokans typically serve kaiseki meals, a multi-course traditional Japanese dinner showcasing seasonal and regional delicacies.

Some ryokans offer special kid-friendly kaiseki meals with milder flavors to suit children's tastes.

4. Futon-Making Experience:

Some ryokans offer a futon-making experience, where children can learn to prepare their futons for bedtime.

5. Yukata (Japanese Robe) Dressing:

Ryokans often provide guests with yukata robes to wear during their stay, creating a cultural and immersive experience.

Children can enjoy dressing up in yukata, making for delightful photo opportunities.

6. Private Dining Areas:

Larger ryokans may offer private dining areas where families can enjoy their meals together in a more intimate setting.

7. Tatami Playrooms:

Some ryokans have designated playrooms with tatami mats where children can play with traditional toys and games.

8. Traditional Garden Views:

Many ryokans have stunning traditional Japanese gardens, providing a serene and picturesque backdrop for the whole family.

9. Cultural Workshops:

Some ryokans offer cultural workshops for guests, including activities like tea ceremonies and origami, providing an opportunity for families to immerse themselves in Japanese traditions.

10. Child-Friendly Amenities:

While ryokans may have a more traditional ambiance, some may also provide baby cots, high chairs, or other child-friendly amenities upon request.

Staying in a traditional ryokan allows families to experience Japan's cultural heritage firsthand and create lasting memories through authentic experiences. Keep in mind that not all ryokans may be suitable for families with young children due to their traditional settings and quiet atmospheres. Before booking a ryokan, it's essential to check their policies and offerings to ensure it aligns with your family's preferences.

Recommended Neighborhoods for Families

Tokyo is a sprawling metropolis with a diverse range of neighborhoods, each offering a unique atmosphere and attractions. When traveling with kids, choosing the right neighborhood can significantly impact your family's experience. Here are some recommended neighborhoods for families visiting Tokyo:

1. Shinjuku:

Shinjuku is a vibrant neighborhood with plenty of family-friendly attractions, including Shinjuku Gyoen National Garden, a beautiful park where kids can run and play.

The area around Shinjuku Station offers excellent shopping and dining options suitable for families.

2. Shibuya:

Shibuya is known for its bustling streets and iconic Shibuya Crossing, which is an exciting sight for kids to experience.

The nearby Yoyogi Park and Meiji Shrine provide green spaces for families to relax and enjoy nature.

3. Ueno:

Ueno is home to Ueno Park, a vast public park with various attractions, including Ueno Zoo and the National Museum of Nature and Science.

The park is an ideal location for family picnics and leisurely walks.

4. Asakusa:

Asakusa offers a glimpse of traditional Tokyo with its historical temples, including the famous Sensō-ji Temple.

Kids can enjoy the bustling atmosphere of Nakamise-dori, a lively shopping street leading to the temple.

5. Odaiba:

Odaiba is a family-friendly entertainment district, offering attractions like TeamLab Borderless, a digital art museum, and the Legoland Discovery Center.

The area features a beach, shopping malls, and waterfront parks.

6. Akihabara:

Akihabara is a paradise for tech-savvy families and fans of anime and gaming.

Kids will be fascinated by the colorful shops and anime-themed cafes.

7. Ikebukuro:

Ikebukuro has several kid-friendly attractions, including Sunshine City, a large entertainment complex with an indoor theme park and aquarium.

The Pokemon Center and Animate store are must-visits for young anime enthusiasts.

8. Roppongi:

Roppongi Hills offers family-friendly attractions like the Mori Art Museum and Tokyo City View Observatory, providing stunning city views.

Kids will enjoy the 360-degree observation deck and interactive exhibits.

9. Ochanomizu:

Ochanomizu is home to the Tokyo Dome City entertainment complex, which includes Tokyo Dome, an amusement park, and a shopping area.

Families can enjoy thrilling rides, live shows, and indoor attractions.

10. Setagaya:

Setagaya is a quieter residential area with several family-friendly parks and playgrounds.

Families seeking a more laid-back atmosphere may find Setagaya appealing.

11. Disney Resort Area:

For families visiting Tokyo Disneyland and Tokyo DisneySea, staying in the Disney Resort Area is a convenient option.

Disney-themed hotels and resorts provide a magical experience for kids.

12. Mitaka:

Mitaka is home to the Ghibli Museum, a must-visit attraction for families who love Studio Ghibli films.

The museum's exhibits and interactive displays enchant both kids and adults.

When selecting a neighborhood to stay in, consider factors such as proximity to family-friendly attractions, ease of access to public transportation, and the overall ambiance. Each neighborhood in Tokyo offers something unique, making it essential to choose one that aligns with your family's interests and preferences.

CHAPTER 3

Exploring Tokyo's Top Attractions

Kid-Friendly Landmarks and Icons

Tokyo, as a bustling metropolis, is home to several iconic landmarks that captivate the imagination of both adults and children alike. These landmarks offer unique experiences and insights into the city's history, culture, and modern advancements. When traveling to Tokyo with kids, visiting these kid-friendly landmarks is a must. Here are three prominent landmarks that will surely leave a lasting impression on your young travelers:

1. Tokyo Tower:

Tokyo Tower is an iconic symbol of the city and a popular destination for families seeking a panoramic view of Tokyo's skyline. Standing at approximately 333 meters (1,093 feet) tall, the tower offers two observation decks with stunning views of the city during the day and a mesmerizing cityscape at night.

Kid-Friendly Activities at Tokyo Tower:

"Lookdown Windows": The observation decks have unique "Lookdown Windows" that allow visitors to view the ground directly below, creating a thrilling experience for kids.

"One Piece Theme Park": At the base of the tower, there is a One Piece theme park for fans of the popular manga and anime series. Kids can meet characters and enjoy interactive exhibits.

Tips for Visiting with Kids:

Visit during the late afternoon to catch both daytime and nighttime views.

Consider using the elevators instead of stairs, especially if you have younger children or strollers.

2. Tokyo Skytree:

Tokyo Skytree is one of the tallest towers in the world, standing at a height of approximately 634 meters (2,080 feet). It offers breathtaking views of Tokyo from its observation decks and has become a prominent landmark in the city since its opening in 2012.

Kid-Friendly Activities at Tokyo Skytree:

"Skytree Town": The lower floors of Tokyo Skytree are home to "Skytree Town," a shopping and entertainment complex with a variety of stores, restaurants, and attractions for kids.

"Sumida Aquarium": Located within Tokyo Skytree Town, this aquarium features a diverse range of marine life and engaging exhibits, making it an excellent place for kids to learn about underwater ecosystems.

Tips for Visiting with Kids:

Consider purchasing tickets in advance to avoid long lines, especially during peak tourist seasons.

Check the weather forecast and visibility conditions before visiting to ensure a clear view from the observation decks.

3. Sensō-ji Temple:

Sensō-ji Temple is an ancient Buddhist temple located in the historic Asakusa district of Tokyo. It is one of the city's most significant cultural landmarks and attracts both tourists and locals seeking spiritual experiences.

Kid-Friendly Activities at Sensō-ji Temple:

"Nakamise Shopping Street": The approach to the temple is lined with Nakamise Shopping Street, offering a variety of traditional snacks, toys, and souvenirs that will intrigue children.

"Omikuji" Fortune-Telling: Kids can participate in the Japanese tradition of drawing "Omikuji" fortune slips at the temple. It's a fun way to learn about Japanese customs.

Tips for Visiting with Kids:

Encourage kids to take part in the cleansing ritual before entering the temple, where they can purify their hands and mouth with water.

Exploring these kid-friendly landmarks in Tokyo will not only provide great photo opportunities but also offer valuable cultural experiences that will enrich your children's understanding of the city and its heritage.

Amusement Parks and Entertainment Centers

Tokyo is a city that knows how to entertain, and it boasts a fantastic array of amusement parks and entertainment centers that cater specifically to kids. From the magic of Disney to the immersive world of KidZania, families can expect a world of excitement and joy. Here are three must-visit amusement parks and entertainment centers in Tokyo:

1. Tokyo Disneyland:

Tokyo Disneyland is a world-renowned theme park and the first Disney park built outside of the United States. It offers a magical experience for families, featuring classic Disney characters, thrilling rides, and enchanting parades.

Kid-Friendly Attractions at Tokyo Disneyland:

"Fantasyland": This area is a favorite among young children with its whimsical attractions like "It's a Small World" and "Pooh's Hunny Hunt."

"Adventureland": Kids can embark on exciting adventures with attractions like "Pirates of the Caribbean" and "Jungle Cruise."

Tips for Visiting with Kids:

Arrive early to maximize your time at the park and experience popular attractions with shorter wait times.

Take advantage of "Disney FASTPASS" to reserve access to certain attractions and reduce wait times.

2. Tokyo DisneySea:

Tokyo DisneySea, located adjacent to Tokyo Disneyland, is a unique and imaginative theme park inspired by myths, legends, and maritime adventures. It offers a more mature atmosphere than Tokyo Disneyland, making it ideal for families with older children.

Kid-Friendly Attractions at Tokyo DisneySea:

"Mermaid Lagoon": This enchanting area is perfect for younger kids, featuring attractions based on "The Little Mermaid."

"Toy Story Mania!": Kids can enjoy interactive 4D shooting games with their favorite Toy Story characters.

Tips for Visiting with Kids:

Allow ample time to explore the park's detailed theming and beautifully designed attractions.

Check the show schedule in advance to catch spectacular live performances.

3. KidZania Tokyo:

KidZania Tokyo is an interactive edutainment center that allows kids to role-play in various professions, from doctors and firefighters to chefs and pilots. It provides a fun and educational environment where children can learn through play.

Activities at KidZania Tokyo:

"Earn KidZos": Kids can participate in activities and earn KidZos, the official currency of KidZania, which they can spend on goods and services within the center.

"KidZania City": The facility recreates a mini city with buildings and establishments, offering a realistic experience for kids.

Tips for Visiting with Kids:

Arrive early to maximize participation in various activities and ensure availability.

Encourage kids to try different roles and activities to broaden their learning experiences.

Visiting these amusement parks and entertainment centers in Tokyo guarantees a day filled with fun, laughter, and unforgettable memories for the whole family.

Interactive Museums and Science Exhibits

For families seeking educational and interactive experiences, Tokyo has a wealth of museums and science exhibits that cater to curious young minds. These institutions offer hands-on learning opportunities and exciting exhibits that spark the imagination. Here are three top-notch interactive museums and science exhibits that kids will adore:

1. National Museum of Nature and Science:

The National Museum of Nature and Science is a fascinating museum that showcases the wonders of the natural world and scientific discoveries. It offers a range of exhibits and interactive displays that engage visitors of all ages.

Interactive Exhibits at the National Museum of Nature and Science:

"Japan Gallery": Kids can explore the geological and ecological diversity of Japan through interactive exhibits and lifelike models of indigenous species.

"Global Gallery": This gallery highlights the broader aspects of the natural world, featuring exhibits on dinosaurs, human evolution, and outer space.

Tips for Visiting with Kids:

Check the museum's schedule for special events and workshops that may enhance your kids' learning experiences.

Participate in guided tours or workshops designed specifically for families.

2. Tokyo National Museum - Heiseikan Kids Plaza:

The Heiseikan Kids Plaza is a section within the Tokyo National Museum that caters specifically to children. It offers interactive exhibits that allow kids to experience traditional Japanese culture, history, and art in a playful and engaging manner.

Interactive Exhibits at Heiseikan Kids Plaza:

"Archeology Exploration Zone": Kids can become archaeologists and discover artifacts from Japan's ancient past in an excavation-themed area.

"Hands-On Experience Workshop": The workshop allows kids to try their hand at traditional crafts and art techniques under the guidance of experts.

Tips for Visiting with Kids:

Combine your visit to Heiseikan Kids Plaza with other sections of the Tokyo National Museum to create a well-rounded cultural experience.

Bring sketchbooks or notebooks for kids to jot down their observations and creative ideas.

3. Miraikan - American Museum of Natural History:

Miraikan, also known as the "Future Museum," is a cutting-edge science museum that focuses on the latest advancements in technology and the exploration of our future.

Interactive Exhibits at Miraikan:

"ASIMO Robot": Witness the humanoid robot ASIMO in action and learn about robotics and artificial intelligence.

"Geo-Cosmos": Marvel at the world's first large-scale spherical OLED screen, displaying real-time global data.

Tips for Visiting with Kids:

Check the schedule for live demonstrations and science shows to enhance the learning experience.

Visit the "Wonder Cockpit" for a simulated space exploration adventure.

These interactive museums and science exhibits provide the perfect combination of education and entertainment, allowing kids to explore the wonders of the natural world and the frontiers of technology in an engaging and enjoyable manner. Visiting these attractions will undoubtedly inspire curiosity and a thirst for knowledge in young minds.

CHAPTER 4

Fun Outdoor Activities

Parks and Gardens for Playtime

Tokyo is a city that values green spaces and offers a wide array of parks and gardens where families can relax, play, and immerse themselves in nature. These serene oases within the bustling metropolis provide a perfect setting for children to run, explore, and have fun. Here are three top parks and gardens in Tokyo that are ideal for playtime with kids:

1. Ueno Park:

Ueno Park is one of Tokyo's most famous and expansive parks, offering a delightful escape from the city's hustle and bustle. It spans over 130 acres and is home to various attractions that cater to families.

Playtime Activities at Ueno Park:

Picnics: Ueno Park is perfect for family picnics, with ample grassy areas and designated picnic spots. Families can enjoy a leisurely meal while surrounded by beautiful cherry blossom trees during the spring.

Playground: The park has several well-equipped playgrounds, including swings, slides, and climbing frames, where children can burn off some energy and make new friends.

Boat Rides: Families can enjoy leisurely boat rides on the park's large pond, offering a serene and picturesque experience.

Family-Friendly Attractions at Ueno Park:

Ueno Zoo: Located within the park, Ueno Zoo is Japan's oldest zoo and features a variety of animals that kids will love to see up close.

Tokyo National Museum: Families can explore Japanese art and history at the Tokyo National Museum, which has kid-friendly exhibits and special events.

Tips for Visiting with Kids:

Visit during the cherry blossom season (late March to early April) for a breathtaking display of cherry blossoms.

Bring a blanket or mat for comfortable seating during picnics.

2. Yoyogi Park:

Yoyogi Park is another expansive green space in Tokyo known for its vast lawns, woodland areas, and vibrant atmosphere. It is a favorite spot for locals and visitors alike, offering various activities for families.

Playtime Activities at Yoyogi Park:

Cycling: Families can rent bicycles and cycle around the park's designated paths, providing a fun and active way to explore the surroundings.

Frisbee and Ball Games: The open lawns of Yoyogi Park are excellent for playing frisbee or ball games, providing plenty of space for kids to run around and enjoy outdoor games.

Rollerblading: Families can rent rollerblades and enjoy gliding through the park's smooth paths.

Family-Friendly Attractions at Yoyogi Park:

Meiji Shrine: Adjacent to Yoyogi Park, the Meiji Shrine is a tranquil Shinto shrine surrounded by lush forest, offering a serene and spiritual experience for families.

Yoyogi National Stadium: Kids interested in sports may enjoy seeing the Yoyogi National Stadium, known for its unique architecture.

Tips for Visiting with Kids:

Check the park's schedule for special events and performances, as Yoyogi Park often hosts live music and cultural festivals.

Consider bringing a ball or frisbee for playtime on the open lawns.

3. Shinjuku Gyoen National Garden:

Shinjuku Gyoen National Garden is a beautiful and serene garden located in the heart of Tokyo. It offers a tranquil escape with various garden styles, including Japanese, English, and French gardens.

Playtime Activities at Shinjuku Gyoen National Garden:

Chasing Koi Fish: The garden's large pond is home to numerous koi fish, and kids can enjoy observing and chasing them along the water's edge.

Nature Walks: Families can take leisurely walks through the picturesque garden paths, enjoying the seasonal blooms and vibrant foliage.

Cherry Blossom Viewing: During the cherry blossom season, the garden becomes a popular spot for hanami (cherry blossom viewing) picnics.

Family-Friendly Attractions at Shinjuku Gyoen National Garden:

Greenhouse: The garden features a greenhouse with tropical and subtropical plants, offering a unique and educational experience for kids.

Tips for Visiting with Kids:

Bring a camera to capture the garden's natural beauty and your kids' joyful moments.

Check the garden's website for seasonal flower bloom schedules, as each season offers a different landscape.

Exploring these parks and gardens with kids not only provides opportunities for play and relaxation but also allows families to connect with nature and experience the serenity of Tokyo's green spaces.

Tokyo Zoo and Aquariums

Tokyo offers a range of zoos and aquariums where families can encounter fascinating wildlife and marine creatures. These facilities provide educational and entertaining experiences for kids, fostering an appreciation for the natural world. Here are two must-visit zoos and aquariums in Tokyo:

1. Ueno Zoo:

Ueno Zoo, located within Ueno Park, is Japan's oldest zoo and houses a diverse collection of animals from around the world. It is a popular destination for families seeking to introduce their kids to various wildlife species.

Kid-Friendly Features at Ueno Zoo:

Panda Exhibit: One of the zoo's main attractions is the Giant Panda exhibit, where kids can see adorable giant pandas up close.

Gorilla Exhibit: Kids will be fascinated by the gorilla enclosure, where they can observe these intelligent and powerful primates.

Educational Programs:

Ueno Zoo offers educational programs and workshops for kids, providing valuable insights into animal behavior, conservation efforts, and wildlife protection.

Tips for Visiting with Kids:

Check the feeding times schedule to witness animals during their most active moments.

Bring binoculars for better views of animals at a distance.

2. Tokyo Sea Life Park:

Tokyo Sea Life Park is a modern and impressive aquarium located in Kasai Rinkai Park. It showcases various marine habitats, from the Tokyo Bay to the deep ocean, allowing families to explore diverse underwater ecosystems.

Kid-Friendly Features at Tokyo Sea Life Park:

Aquatic Tunnel: The aquarium's main attraction is the impressive aquatic tunnel, where families can walk through a transparent tube surrounded by marine life swimming overhead.

Interactive Touch Pools: Kids can touch and interact with various sea creatures in designated touch pools, providing a hands-on learning experience.

Educational Programs:

Tokyo Sea Life Park offers educational programs and marine-themed workshops for kids to learn about ocean conservation and marine biodiversity.

Tips for Visiting with Kids:

Avoid visiting during weekends and holidays to minimize crowds.

Allow sufficient time to explore all the exhibits and attend scheduled shows and feedings.

Visiting Tokyo's zoos and aquariums not only offers an enjoyable day out for families but also fosters a sense of responsibility and care for the natural world in young children.

Boat Cruises and Sumida River Adventures

Exploring Tokyo from the water offers a unique perspective and a refreshing experience for families. Several boat cruises and tours provide an exciting way to see the city's iconic landmarks and scenic views along the Sumida River. Here's a captivating boat adventure for families in Tokyo:

1. Sumida River Boat Cruises:

The Sumida River flows through Tokyo, and various boat companies offer scenic cruises that take passengers on a journey through the heart of the city. These cruises provide an opportunity to see Tokyo's skyline and famous landmarks from a different angle.

Kid-Friendly Highlights of Sumida River Cruises:

Tokyo Skytree Views: Cruises along the Sumida River offer fantastic views of Tokyo Skytree, one of the city's most iconic structures.

Rainbow Bridge: Some cruises extend to Tokyo Bay, where families can enjoy views of the illuminated Rainbow Bridge at night.

Cruise Options:

Daytime Cruises: Daytime cruises are ideal for families who want to appreciate Tokyo's cityscape and landmarks under natural lighting.

Night Cruises: Night cruises create a magical ambiance, with city lights illuminating the riverbanks and landmarks.

Tips for Boat Cruises with Kids:

Check the schedule and availability of cruises, as some cruises may have limited departure times.

Bring snacks and drinks to keep kids entertained during the cruise.

Boat cruises on the Sumida River offer a memorable and picturesque way to explore Tokyo's landscape, and they are particularly enjoyable for kids who love being on the water and marveling at the city's impressive architecture.

CHAPTER 5

Family-Friendly Dining

Introduction to Japanese Cuisine for Kids

One of the most exciting aspects of traveling to Tokyo with kids is the opportunity to introduce them to Japanese cuisine. Japanese food is not only delicious but also visually appealing, making it an ideal culinary adventure for young taste buds. From sushi to tempura and delightful desserts, there is a wide array of flavors and textures to explore. Here's an introduction to some popular Japanese dishes and treats that kids are sure to enjoy:

1. Sushi:

Sushi is perhaps the most iconic Japanese dish known worldwide. It consists of vinegared rice topped with various ingredients, such as raw fish (sashimi), cooked seafood, vegetables, or egg. For kids who may be hesitant about raw fish, there are plenty of sushi options that include cooked ingredients like shrimp, crab, or tamago (sweet rolled omelet).

Kid-Friendly Sushi Rolls:

California Roll: This roll contains imitation crab meat, avocado, and cucumber, making it a favorite among kids.

Tamago Nigiri: Sweet and fluffy rolled omelet served on a small mound of rice, which is a simple and delightful sushi option for children.

2. Tempura:

Tempura is a popular Japanese dish consisting of lightly battered and deep-fried seafood or vegetables. The light and crispy texture make it appealing to kids, and it's often served with a dipping sauce for added flavor.

Kid-Friendly Tempura Options:

Shrimp Tempura: Crispy shrimp tempura is a favorite among kids due to its crunchy exterior and tender inside.

Vegetable Tempura: Various vegetables like sweet potatoes, zucchini, and pumpkin are lightly fried to create delicious tempura options for kids.

3. Ramen:

Ramen is a hearty and comforting noodle soup, featuring wheat noodles served in a flavorful broth, typically topped with slices of pork, green onions, and other garnishes. There are different types of ramen, with various broth flavors to suit different preferences.

Kid-Friendly Ramen Types:

Shoyu Ramen: A soy sauce-based broth with a mild and familiar taste that kids may enjoy.

Miso Ramen: A broth made from fermented soybean paste, providing a rich and slightly sweet flavor that kids find delicious.

4. Okonomiyaki:

Okonomiyaki is a savory pancake filled with various ingredients such as cabbage, meat, seafood, and topped with savory sauce and mayonnaise. It's often cooked on a grill right at the table, creating an interactive dining experience for kids.

Kid-Friendly Okonomiyaki:

Cheese Okonomiyaki: A kid-friendly version that includes melted cheese, adding a gooey and flavorful twist to the dish.

5. Gyoza:

Gyoza are Japanese dumplings filled with minced meat and vegetables, often pan-fried to achieve a crispy texture. They are a favorite appetizer for kids and can be dipped in a tangy sauce for extra flavor.

Kid-Friendly Gyoza Dipping Sauce:

A simple mixture of soy sauce and vinegar, sometimes with a touch of chili oil, offers a dipping sauce with kid-approved flavors.

6. Takoyaki:

Takoyaki are savory octopus-filled balls made from a batter of flour, eggs, and dashi (a Japanese stock). They are cooked in special round molds, resulting in delicious bite-sized snacks that kids enjoy.

Kid-Friendly Takoyaki Variation:

Cheese Takoyaki: A version with melted cheese filling, creating a gooey and tasty center that kids love.

7. Japanese Desserts:

Japanese desserts are not only delectable but also aesthetically pleasing. From delicate wagashi (traditional Japanese sweets) to fluffy Japanese cheesecake and matcha-flavored treats, there are plenty of sweet options for kids to try.

Kid-Friendly Japanese Desserts:

Taiyaki: Fish-shaped cake filled with sweet red bean paste or custard, providing a delightful treat for kids.

Mochi Ice Cream: Soft and chewy rice cake filled with ice cream in various flavors, offering a unique and enjoyable dessert experience.

Introducing kids to Japanese cuisine can be a delightful journey of flavors and textures, providing them with a sense of culinary adventure and cultural exploration during their time in Tokyo.

Kid-Friendly Restaurants and Food Options

Traveling with kids often involves seeking out restaurants that cater to young diners, offer kid-friendly menus, and provide a welcoming ambiance for families. Tokyo is a family-friendly city, and there are plenty of restaurants and food options that ensure an enjoyable dining experience for kids. Here are some types of eateries and food choices that kids are sure to love:

1. Conveyor Belt Sushi (Kaiten-zushi) Restaurants:

Conveyor belt sushi, also known as kaiten-zushi, is a fun and interactive dining experience that appeals to children and adults alike. In these restaurants, plates of sushi rotate on a conveyor belt, allowing diners to pick and choose their favorite dishes as they pass by.

Kid-Friendly Aspects of Conveyor Belt Sushi Restaurants:

Visual Appeal: The colorful and eye-catching sushi plates rotating on the conveyor belt captivate children's attention and make dining exciting.

Self-Service: Kids can pick their favorite sushi dishes directly from the conveyor belt, giving them a sense of independence and control over their meal choices.

Kid-Friendly Sushi Choices:

Sushi with Cooked Ingredients: Conveyor belt sushi restaurants offer a variety of sushi with cooked ingredients, such as tempura shrimp, cooked salmon, and tamago (rolled sweet omelet), which are ideal options for kids who may be hesitant about raw fish.

2. Themed Cafes and Restaurants:

Tokyo is famous for its themed cafes and restaurants, where the dining experience is elevated to a whole new level with creative and whimsical themes. These themed eateries often feature decor, dishes, and performances related to a specific concept, character, or anime.

Kid-Friendly Themed Cafes and Restaurants:

Character Cafes: Themed cafes based on popular characters from anime, manga, and video games offer a magical and immersive experience for kids.

Animal Cafes: Cafes where kids can interact with cute animals, such as cats, owls, and hedgehogs, create unforgettable memories.

Kid-Friendly Themes:

Hello Kitty Cafe: A beloved character-themed cafe that appeals to kids of all ages with its adorable and pink-themed decor.

Pokemon Cafe: A must-visit for Pokemon fans, where kids can enjoy Pokemon-themed dishes and meet Pikachu.

3. Street Food Delights:

Tokyo's vibrant street food scene offers a wide array of delectable treats that kids will find irresistible. Exploring food stalls and street vendors is an adventure in itself, allowing kids to sample a variety of Japanese snacks and treats.

Kid-Friendly Street Food Delights:

Takoyaki: Savory octopus-filled balls topped with savory sauce and mayonnaise are a popular street food option that kids enjoy.

Taiyaki: Fish-shaped cakes filled with sweet red bean paste or custard are a delightful and portable treat for kids on the go.

Tips for Enjoying Street Food with Kids:

Consider portion sizes and choose snacks that are easy for kids to handle and eat while walking.

4. Kid-Friendly Bento Boxes:

Bento boxes are a quintessential part of Japanese cuisine and are perfect for kids as they offer a well-balanced and visually appealing meal in a compact package.

Kid-Friendly Bento Options:

Katsu Bento: Bento boxes featuring breaded and fried cutlets (katsu) of chicken, pork, or fish are a hit with kids due to their crunchy texture.

Tamago Sushi Bento: Bento boxes with various tamago (rolled sweet omelet) sushi options are both delicious and visually appealing to kids.

Tips for Choosing Kid-Friendly Bento Boxes:

Look for bento boxes with a variety of colors and shapes, as visual appeal plays a crucial role in enticing kids to try new foods. Opt for bento boxes with familiar ingredients and flavors that align with kids' preferences. Introducing kids to a variety of dining experiences, from interactive sushi restaurants to whimsical themed cafes and delicious street food, enhances their culinary exploration and cultural appreciation during their Tokyo adventure.

CHAPTER 6

Tokyo's Hidden Gems

Quirky and Unique Spots Loved by Kids

Tokyo is a city full of surprises and unique attractions that cater to the imaginations of kids. From whimsical museums to fascinating themed spots, there are plenty of quirky places that will capture the hearts of young travelers. Here are four quirky and unique spots loved by kids in Tokyo:

1. Ghibli Museum:

The Ghibli Museum is a must-visit for families, especially if your kids are fans of Studio Ghibli films. Studio Ghibli is renowned for producing animated masterpieces such as "My Neighbor Totoro," "Spirited Away," and "Howl's Moving Castle." The museum is dedicated to showcasing the art, animation, and creativity behind these beloved films.

Highlights of the Ghibli Museum:

Film Exhibitions: The museum features rotating exhibits that allow visitors to explore the behind-the-scenes process of creating Studio Ghibli's films.

Catbus Room: Kids can climb and play inside a life-size replica of the Catbus from "My Neighbor Totoro," adding to the sense of wonder and magic.

Tips for Visiting with Kids:

Purchase tickets in advance, as entry is limited and tickets often sell out quickly.

Allow plenty of time to explore the exhibits and enjoy the immersive experience.

2. Fire Museum (Taito Ryokan):

The Fire Museum, also known as Taito Ryokan, is a quirky and interactive museum that educates visitors about fire safety in an entertaining way. The museum is housed in a former fire station and features various exhibits, hands-on activities, and firefighting equipment.

Kid-Friendly Features of the Fire Museum:

Fire Truck Rides: Kids can experience the thrill of riding on a real fire truck, giving them a taste of what it's like to be a firefighter.

Interactive Exhibits: The museum offers interactive exhibits where kids can role-play as firefighters and learn about fire safety.

Tips for Visiting with Kids:

The museum may get crowded on weekends and holidays, so consider visiting on weekdays for a more relaxed experience.

Engage with the hands-on activities and encourage kids to participate in the interactive exhibits.

3. Tokyo Toy Museum:

The Tokyo Toy Museum is a delightful place that transports kids into the enchanting world of toys. The museum showcases a vast collection of vintage and contemporary toys from Japan and around the world, making it a treasure trove of playtime memories.

Kid-Friendly Activities at the Toy Museum:

Playroom Zones: The museum has playroom zones with various types of toys, including building blocks, dolls, and board games, where kids can engage in creative play.

Toy Workshops: The museum occasionally hosts workshops where kids can make their own toys and crafts.

Tips for Visiting with Kids:

Check the museum's schedule for special events and workshops that may enhance your kids' experience.

Allow ample time for kids to explore the playrooms and engage with different toys.

4. TeamLab Borderless:

TeamLab Borderless is an innovative and immersive digital art museum that combines technology, art, and interactive experiences. The museum features stunning digital installations that respond to visitors' movements, creating a mesmerizing and dreamlike atmosphere.

Kid-Friendly Features of TeamLab Borderless:

Interactive Artworks: Kids can explore various interactive installations, such as a digital waterfall room and a mesmerizing floating flower garden.

Athletic Forest: The museum's Athletic Forest is an area where kids can play and interact with digital animals and creatures.

Tips for Visiting with Kids:

Plan your visit on weekdays to avoid larger crowds and ensure a more relaxed experience.

Wear comfortable clothing, as kids may be running and moving around while exploring the interactive artworks.

Off-the-Beaten-Path Parks and Playgrounds

While Tokyo is known for its bustling cityscape, it also offers hidden gems in the form of off-the-beaten-path parks and playgrounds where kids can run, play, and explore. These lesser-known parks provide a welcome break from the city's hustle and allow families to connect with nature. Here are three off-the-beaten-path parks and playgrounds loved by kids:

1. Todoroki Valley:

Todoroki Valley is a peaceful oasis in the Setagaya ward of Tokyo, offering a serene and natural environment for families to unwind and reconnect with nature. The valley features a gentle stream, walking paths, and lush greenery, providing an ideal setting for a leisurely stroll or a family picnic.

Family-Friendly Activities at Todoroki Valley:

Exploring the Stream: Kids can splash and play in the shallow stream that flows through the valley, creating a refreshing and immersive experience.

Todoroki Fudoson Temple: The valley leads to Todoroki Fudoson, a Buddhist temple with a calming atmosphere, perfect for a moment of tranquility.

Tips for Visiting with Kids:

Wear comfortable shoes suitable for walking on the forested paths.

Bring a small net for kids to catch tadpoles or small fish in the stream.

2. Arisugawa-no-miya Memorial Park:

Arisugawa-no-miya Memorial Park, located in the Azabu-Juban neighborhood, is a serene and charming park that offers a variety of play areas and open spaces for families to enjoy.

Kid-Friendly Features of Arisugawa-no-miya Memorial Park:

Playground Areas: The park has well-equipped playgrounds with swings, slides, and climbing structures, providing hours of fun for kids.

Pond and Ducks: Kids can feed ducks and enjoy watching turtles in the park's picturesque pond.

Tips for Visiting with Kids:

Pack a picnic and enjoy a meal on the park's grassy areas.

Visit during the cherry blossom season for a picturesque view of cherry blossoms in bloom.

3. Showa Memorial Park (Showa Kinen Park):

Showa Memorial Park is a vast and expansive park located in Tachikawa City, offering a diverse range of activities and recreational facilities for families. The park's large size provides ample space for kids to run, play, and explore.

Family-Friendly Activities at Showa Memorial Park:

Cycling: Families can rent bicycles and explore the park's numerous cycling paths, providing an active and enjoyable way to see the park's attractions.

Adventure Playground: The park features an adventure playground with exciting play structures, slides, and climbing walls for kids to enjoy.

Tips for Visiting with Kids:

Rent a pedal-powered cart for a fun and unique way to explore the park.

Check the park's calendar for special events and festivals that may coincide with your visit.

Exploring these off-the-beaten-path parks and playgrounds allows families to escape the bustling city and immerse themselves in tranquil and natural settings. These hidden gems offer a chance for kids to play freely and make unforgettable memories amidst the beauty of Tokyo's green spaces.

CHAPTER 7

Seasonal Festivities and Events

Cherry Blossom Viewing (Hanami) Spots

Cherry blossom season, also known as hanami, is one of the most anticipated times of the year in Tokyo. The blooming of cherry blossoms marks the arrival of spring and is a cherished tradition in Japan. Families can partake in this beautiful cultural experience by visiting some of the best cherry blossom viewing spots in Tokyo. Here are four hanami spots loved by kids:

1. Ueno Park:

Ueno Park is a top destination for cherry blossom viewing in Tokyo. With over 1,000 cherry trees lining its pathways, the park transforms into a breathtaking sea of pink during the cherry blossom season. Families can enjoy hanami picnics under the blossoms while admiring the cultural performances and festivities that often take place in the park.

Kid-Friendly Activities at Ueno Park:

Boat Rides: Rent a rowboat or swan boat to cruise along the park's Shinobazu Pond, providing kids with a unique view of the cherry blossoms from the water.

Tokyo National Museum: While at Ueno Park, consider visiting the Tokyo National Museum, which often hosts kid-friendly exhibitions and events during the cherry blossom season.

Tips for Visiting with Kids:

Arrive early to secure a good spot for your hanami picnic, as Ueno Park can get crowded during peak cherry blossom season.

Bring a picnic blanket and some snacks for a leisurely and enjoyable day under the cherry blossoms.

2. Shinjuku Gyoen National Garden:

Shinjuku Gyoen is another must-visit hanami spot, known for its stunning cherry blossom displays. The garden offers a serene and picturesque environment for families to immerse themselves in the beauty of the cherry blossoms. With various cherry tree varieties, the bloom season at Shinjuku Gyoen can extend longer than in other parks.

Kid-Friendly Activities at Shinjuku Gyoen National Garden:

Explore the Greenhouse: Visit the greenhouse, where kids can learn about various plant species and observe tropical and subtropical plants.

Picnic and Playgrounds: Shinjuku Gyoen has several designated picnic areas and playgrounds, providing kids with opportunities to play amidst the cherry blossoms.

Tips for Visiting with Kids:

Check the garden's website or information center for cherry blossom bloom updates to plan your visit accordingly.

Consider renting bicycles to explore the vast garden with kids, making it easier for them to cover more ground and see different cherry blossom areas.

3. Sumida Park:

Located along the Sumida River, Sumida Park offers a stunning backdrop for cherry blossom viewing. Families can enjoy leisurely strolls along the riverbank, taking in the views of cherry blossoms in full bloom while appreciating the iconic Tokyo Skytree in the distance.

Kid-Friendly Activities at Sumida Park:

Tokyo Water Bus: Take a Tokyo Water Bus ride along the Sumida River to enjoy the cherry blossoms from a different perspective.

Hanami Boat Cruises: Some boat operators offer hanami boat cruises specifically for cherry blossom viewing, which can be a delightful experience for kids.

Tips for Visiting with Kids:

Consider combining your visit to Sumida Park with a trip to Tokyo Skytree, where kids can enjoy panoramic views of Tokyo from the observation deck.

Bring a camera to capture the scenic beauty of the cherry blossoms along the Sumida River.

4. Chidorigafuchi:

Chidorigafuchi is a picturesque area surrounding the moat of the Imperial Palace, and it is famous for its cherry blossom-lined walking paths. Families can rent rowboats to row through the enchanting tunnel of cherry blossoms, creating a magical and unforgettable experience for kids.

Kid-Friendly Activities at Chidorigafuchi:

Rowboat Rental: Renting rowboats allows kids to actively participate in the hanami experience while rowing through the breathtaking cherry blossom tunnel.

Tips for Visiting with Kids:

Rowboat rentals can be in high demand during peak cherry blossom season, so consider arriving early or checking the rental schedule in advance.

Keep in mind that rowboats have limited capacity, so plan accordingly if you have a larger family group.

Summer Festivals (Matsuri) for Kids

Summer in Tokyo is synonymous with vibrant festivals known as matsuri. These traditional festivals celebrate Japanese culture, heritage, and local communities. Participating in a summer matsuri is a fantastic way for families to immerse themselves in the lively atmosphere and enjoy traditional performances, food stalls, and games. Here are four summer festivals loved by kids in Tokyo:

1. Asakusa Samba Carnival:

The Asakusa Samba Carnival is a lively and colorful event that takes place in August in Asakusa, Tokyo. This unique carnival brings the vibrant spirit of Rio de Janeiro's Carnival to the streets of Tokyo. Families can watch dazzling samba performances by costumed dancers and musicians as they parade through the Asakusa district.

Kid-Friendly Aspects of Asakusa Samba Carnival:

Colorful Costumes: The extravagant costumes and vibrant colors will captivate kids' attention, creating a festive and joyful atmosphere.

Street Performances: Various street performers and entertainers add to the excitement, ensuring that there is something to delight every member of the family.

Tips for Attending with Kids:

The carnival can get crowded, so consider arriving early to secure a good viewing spot.

Stay hydrated and bring snacks for kids to enjoy during the parade.

2. Sumida River Fireworks Festival:

The Sumida River Fireworks Festival, known as Sumidagawa Hanabi Taikai, is one of Tokyo's most famous and spectacular fireworks displays. Held in late July, families gather along the Sumida River to watch thousands of fireworks light up the night sky in a mesmerizing symphony of colors.

Kid-Friendly Aspects of the Fireworks Festival:

Dazzling Fireworks: Kids will be awestruck by the breathtaking fireworks display, featuring various shapes and colors illuminating the sky.

Festival Food Stalls: The festival offers a wide variety of traditional Japanese festival foods that kids can enjoy, such as yakitori (grilled skewers), takoyaki (octopus balls), and shaved ice.

Tips for Attending with Kids:

The celebration draws many of people, so get there early to get a good place along the riverfront.

Bring a picnic blanket for a comfortable and enjoyable viewing experience with the family.

3. Mitama Matsuri at Yasukuni Shrine:

The Mitama Matsuri is held in July at the Yasukuni Shrine and is known for its mesmerizing display of lanterns. The festival features around 30,000 paper lanterns, creating a serene and spiritual atmosphere. Families can stroll along the lantern-lit paths and participate in traditional ceremonies.

Kid-Friendly Aspects of Mitama Matsuri:

Lantern Display: Kids will be fascinated by the thousands of lanterns, creating a magical ambiance that is both captivating and calming.

Yukata Rentals: Families can rent yukata, traditional summer kimonos, for kids to wear during the festival, adding to the cultural experience.

Tips for Attending with Kids:

The festival takes place in the evening, so plan accordingly for kids' bedtime and ensure they are well-rested for the experience.

Encourage kids to participate in traditional ceremonies, such as writing wishes on wooden prayer plaques.

4. Koenji Awa Odori:

The Koenji Awa Odori is a lively and energetic dance festival held in August in the bohemian neighborhood of Koenji. The festival features various dance troupes performing traditional Awa Odori dances, and spectators are encouraged to join in the festivities.

Kid-Friendly Aspects of Koenji Awa Odori:

Energetic Performances: Kids will enjoy watching the lively performances and may even be inspired to join the dancers in the festival procession.

Street Food Stalls: The festival offers a variety of delicious street food options, making it a perfect opportunity for kids to try new and exciting flavors.

Tips for Attending with Kids:

The festival can get crowded, so consider arriving early to find a good viewing spot along the parade route.

Encourage kids to participate in the dance and embrace the festive spirit of the event.

Winter Illuminations and Christmas Markets

Tokyo comes alive with a dazzling display of winter illuminations and festive Christmas markets during the holiday season. These enchanting displays of lights and seasonal festivities add a touch of magic to the city's winter atmosphere. Here are three winter attractions loved by kids in Tokyo:

1. Tokyo Midtown Winter Illumination:

Tokyo Midtown is known for its grand and elaborate winter illuminations, attracting families from all over the city. The light displays feature various themes and installations that create a mesmerizing wonderland for kids to explore.

Kid-Friendly Aspects of Tokyo Midtown Winter Illumination:

Light Tunnel: Kids will be thrilled to walk through the illuminated light tunnel, which feels like stepping into a fairy tale world.

Kids' Ice Skating Rink: The winter illumination event often includes an ice skating rink specifically for kids, providing a fun and festive activity.

Tips for Visiting with Kids:

Check the event's schedule for special performances and events that may appeal to kids.

Dress warmly, as the temperatures can be chilly in the evening.

2. Caretta Shiodome Winter Illumination:

Caretta Shiodome, a shopping and entertainment complex, hosts an annual winter illumination event that is nothing short of breathtaking. The highlight of the display is the impressive light show set to music, creating a delightful and captivating experience for visitors.

Kid-Friendly Aspects of Caretta Shiodome Winter Illumination:

Illuminated Show: Kids will be mesmerized by the coordinated light show, which often features popular characters and themes.

Shopping and Dining: Caretta Shiodome offers a range of shopping and dining options, making it a convenient place for families to spend an evening.

Tips for Visiting with Kids:

Arrive a little early to find a good spot to watch the light show, as it can get crowded during peak hours.

Consider visiting the adjacent Shiodome City Center for more winter illumination displays and photo opportunities.

3. Christmas Markets:

During the holiday season, Tokyo is home to several charming Christmas markets that exude a festive and cozy atmosphere. These markets offer a delightful experience for families, with festive decorations, food stalls, and handcrafted gifts.

Kid-Friendly Aspects of Christmas Markets:

Santa Claus: Many Christmas markets feature Santa Claus, allowing kids to meet the jolly old man in person and share their Christmas wishes.

Seasonal Treats: Kids can enjoy seasonal treats like hot cocoa, roasted chestnuts, and gingerbread cookies, adding to the festive experience.

Tips for Visiting Christmas Markets with Kids:

Check the market's schedule for special events and activities that may appeal to kids.

Encourage kids to browse the handcrafted stalls for unique and meaningful gifts.

CHAPTER 8

Shopping with Kids

Souvenirs and Keepsakes

Souvenirs play a significant role in any travel experience, and Tokyo offers a plethora of unique and culturally rich keepsakes that kids can treasure as memories of their trip. From traditional crafts to modern pop-culture items, there is a wide variety of souvenirs to choose from. Here are some must-visit places for finding the perfect souvenirs and keepsakes for kids in Tokyo:

1. Asakusa Nakamise Shopping Street:

Asakusa Nakamise is a vibrant shopping street that leads to Senso-ji Temple, one of Tokyo's oldest and most significant temples. The street is lined with an array of shops selling traditional Japanese souvenirs, snacks, and handicrafts.

Popular Souvenirs at Asakusa Nakamise:

Omamori: Omamori are traditional Japanese amulets that provide protection and good luck. Kids can choose from various omamori, such as those for good grades, safe travels, or success in sports.

Yukata: Yukata are lightweight summer kimonos that kids can wear during festivals and events. They have a wide range of vivid colors and designs.

Tips for Shopping with Kids at Asakusa Nakamise:

Let kids explore the shops and choose souvenirs that catch their eye, empowering them to make their own selections.

Consider getting a traditional omikuji (fortune-telling paper) for each child, adding an element of excitement to the shopping experience.

2. Tokyo Character Street at Tokyo Station:

Located within Tokyo Station, Tokyo Character Street is a shopping area dedicated to character merchandise from popular anime, manga, and video game franchises. It's a haven for kids who are fans of Japanese pop culture.

Popular Character Merchandise at Tokyo Character Street:

Plush Toys: Kids can find a wide selection of plush toys featuring beloved characters from anime and manga series.

Stationery: Character-themed stationery, including notebooks, pens, and stickers, are popular among young anime fans.

Tips for Shopping with Kids at Tokyo Character Street:

Prepare a budget for souvenir shopping and let kids manage their spending while choosing items they love.

Check the schedule for any special events or character appearances that may coincide with your visit.

3. Tokyo Solamachi at Tokyo Skytree:

Tokyo Solamachi is a shopping complex located at the base of Tokyo Skytree, offering a wide range of shops and restaurants. The mall includes several floors dedicated to souvenirs and gifts, making it a convenient one-stop-shop for kids' keepsakes.

Popular Souvenirs at Tokyo Solamachi:

Tokyo Skytree Merchandise: Look for Tokyo Skytree-themed items such as keychains, magnets, and T-shirts featuring the iconic landmark.

Japanese Snacks: Tokyo Solamachi offers an extensive selection of Japanese snacks and treats that make great gifts for friends and family back home.

Tips for Shopping with Kids at Tokyo Solamachi:

Take a break at one of the mall's kid-friendly cafes or eateries to recharge during your shopping spree.

Look for souvenirs that reflect kids' interests, whether it's cute characters, traditional crafts, or fun snacks.

4. Akihabara:

Akihabara, also known as Electric Town, is a mecca for electronics, anime, and gaming enthusiasts. While it's known for its tech shops, it also offers a treasure trove of anime merchandise and unique souvenirs.

Popular Souvenirs in Akihabara:

Anime Figurines: Akihabara boasts a vast selection of anime figurines and collectibles that will delight anime fans of all ages.

Manga and Light Novels: Kids can find the latest manga volumes and light novels from their favorite series.

Tips for Shopping with Kids in Akihabara:

If kids are into video games, consider looking for retro gaming shops that sell vintage consoles and games as special souvenirs.

Many shops in Akihabara offer tax-free shopping for tourists, so don't forget to bring your passport for additional savings.

Toy Stores and Anime Merchandise

For kids who love toys, action figures, and all things anime-related, Tokyo is a paradise. The city is home to numerous toy stores and specialty shops that cater to the diverse interests of young enthusiasts. Here are some must-visit places for kids to indulge in their toy and anime cravings:

1. Kiddy Land in Harajuku:

Kiddy Land is a renowned toy store in Harajuku, offering six floors of toys, character merchandise, and games. Each floor is dedicated to a different theme, providing a delightful shopping experience for kids.

Highlights of Kiddy Land:

Character Merchandise: Kiddy Land has an extensive selection of character-themed toys, stationery, and accessories featuring popular anime and cartoon characters.

Interactive Displays: Many sections of Kiddy Land have interactive displays that allow kids to play and interact with the toys before making a purchase.

Tips for Visiting Kiddy Land with Kids:

Let kids explore each floor at their own pace, as they may want to spend more time in certain sections that pique their interests.

Look out for special events or limited-edition merchandise releases that may coincide with your visit.

2. Mandarake in Akihabara:

Mandarake is a famous retailer specializing in used manga, anime goods, and vintage toys. It's a treasure trove for collectors and kids who enjoy exploring unique and rare finds.

Highlights of Mandarake:

Rare Collectibles: Mandarake often has rare and vintage toys and collectibles from classic anime series that may not be found elsewhere.

Used Manga and Artbooks: Kids can find a wide selection of used manga and artbooks at more affordable prices.

Tips for Visiting Mandarake with Kids:

Encourage kids to browse the shelves and explore the wide array of products, as there may be hidden gems waiting to be discovered.

While Mandarake is a paradise for anime enthusiasts, some sections may have collectibles that are more suitable for older kids, so keep an eye on their selections.

3. Sunshine City: Pokemon Center Tokyo DX:

Sunshine City in Ikebukuro is a massive shopping and entertainment complex, and it houses the Pokemon Center Tokyo DX, a dream destination for Pokemon fans.

Highlights of Pokemon Center Tokyo DX:

Exclusive Merchandise: The store offers exclusive Pokemon merchandise and limited-edition items that can't be found elsewhere.

Photo Opportunities: Kids can take photos with life-size Pikachu and other beloved Pokemon mascots.

Tips for Visiting Pokemon Center Tokyo DX with Kids:

Set a budget beforehand to avoid overspending on all the adorable Pokemon merchandise.

Look for interactive displays and mini-games that kids can enjoy within the store.

4. Character Street at Tokyo Station:

In addition to Tokyo Character Street, Tokyo Station's underground shopping area, known as Character Street, offers even more character merchandise shops for kids to explore.

Highlights of Character Street:

Diverse Characters: Character Street features shops dedicated to various popular anime, manga, and game characters, providing a wide range of choices for kids.

Tokyo Station Souvenirs: Kids can find unique Tokyo Station-themed merchandise that serves as both a souvenir and a memory of their time in the city.

Tips for Visiting Character Street with Kids:

Take breaks at the various cafes and eateries along Character Street to rest and recharge.

Consider purchasing character-themed snacks and treats as gifts for friends and family back home.

Kid-Friendly Shopping Malls

Tokyo's shopping malls offer much more than just retail therapy; they are family-friendly destinations with a diverse range of entertainment and dining options. From indoor amusement parks to interactive play areas, here are some kid-friendly shopping malls where families can shop, play, and dine together:

1. DiverCity Tokyo Plaza:

DiverCity Tokyo Plaza, located in Odaiba, is a shopping mall known for its Gundam Front Tokyo and indoor amusement park, Tokyo Joypolis. It's an ideal destination for families with kids of all ages.

Highlights of DiverCity Tokyo Plaza:

Gundam Front Tokyo: Kids can explore the world of Gundam, a famous Japanese robot franchise, and take photos with life-size Gundam statues.

Tokyo Joypolis: Tokyo Joypolis is an indoor amusement park offering a variety of rides and interactive attractions, providing hours of entertainment for kids.

Tips for Visiting DiverCity Tokyo Plaza with Kids:

Check the schedules for special Gundam shows and events that may coincide with your visit.

Purchase an all-day pass for Tokyo Joypolis to make the most of the indoor amusement park experience.

2. Lalaport Tokyo Bay:

Lalaport Tokyo Bay, located near Tokyo Disneyland, is a large shopping mall with a wide selection of shops, restaurants, and entertainment facilities for kids.

Highlights of Lalaport Tokyo Bay:

Kid-O-Kid: Kid-O-Kid is an expansive indoor playground and play area with activities suitable for younger children.

Cinema Complex: Families can enjoy the latest movie releases at the mall's cinema complex after a day of shopping and play.

Tips for Visiting Lalaport Tokyo Bay with Kids:

Plan your visit to coincide with Kid-O-Kid's daily schedule, as there may be special events and shows that kids can enjoy.

Take advantage of family-friendly dining options in the mall's food court for a quick and convenient meal.

3. Tokyo Midtown:

Tokyo Midtown, located in Roppongi, is not just a shopping complex but also a cultural hub with art galleries, green spaces, and seasonal events that cater to families.

Highlights of Tokyo Midtown:

Midtown Garden: Tokyo Midtown's spacious garden area offers a tranquil space for kids to run and play amidst greenery.

Midtown Ice Rink (Seasonal): During the winter months, the Midtown Ice Rink provides a fun and festive ice skating experience for kids.

Tips for Visiting Tokyo Midtown with Kids:

Check the event schedule for any seasonal events or exhibitions that may be of interest to kids.

Take a leisurely stroll through the garden to enjoy the natural beauty of the surroundings.

4. Aqua City Odaiba:

Aqua City Odaiba is a shopping and entertainment complex located in Odaiba, known for its stunning views of Tokyo Bay and the Rainbow Bridge.

Highlights of Aqua City Odaiba:

Legoland Discovery Center: Aqua City is home to the Legoland Discovery Center, offering Lego-themed rides, play zones, and interactive activities for kids.

Tokyo Trick Art Museum: Kids can have fun interacting with optical illusion artworks at the Tokyo Trick Art Museum.

Tips for Visiting Aqua City Odaiba with Kids:

Purchase tickets for the Legoland Discovery Center in advance to avoid long queues.

Capture the scenic views of Tokyo Bay and the Rainbow Bridge from the observation decks at Aqua City.

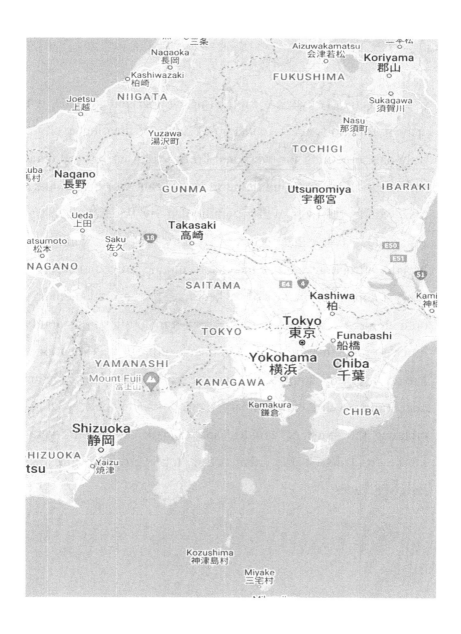

MAP OF TOKYO

CONCLUSION

In conclusion, Tokyo is a captivating wonderland for kids, where ancient traditions meet modern pop culture, creating a city that truly has something for everyone. From exploring historic temples and beautiful parks to indulging in the vibrant world of anime and toys, young travelers will be enthralled by the rich tapestry of experiences Tokyo has to offer. The city's warm hospitality, kid-friendly attractions, and abundance of unique souvenirs ensure that every moment spent in Tokyo becomes a treasured memory for both children and their families. Tokyo's magic lies in its ability to ignite the imaginations of the young, making it a destination that leaves a lasting impression and beckons them back for more adventures in this extraordinary metropolis. So, pack your bags, embrace the spirit of wonder, and embark on an unforgettable journey to Tokyo – a city that is truly a playground of dreams for kids of all ages.

Made in the USA
Las Vegas, NV
15 February 2024

85810509R00066